The Coat

Sharon Holt
Connah Brecon

NELSON
CENGAGE Learning™

Australia • Brazil • Japan • Korea • Mexico • Singapore • Spain • United Kingdom • United States

The Coat

Fast Forward
Purple Level 20

Text: Sharon Holt
Illustrations: Connah Brecon
Editor: Cameron Macintosh
Design: Mandi Cole
Series design: James Lowe
Production controller: Seona Galbally
Audio recordings: Juliet Hill, Picture Start
Spoken by: Matthew King and Abbe Holmes
Reprint: Jennifer Foo

ISBN 978 0 17 012661 8
ISBN 978 0 17 012657 1 (set)

Cengage Learning Australia
Level 7, 80 Dorcas Street
South Melbourne, Victoria Australia 3205
Phone: 1300 790 853

Cengage Learning New Zealand
Unit 4B Rosedale Office Park
331 Rosedale Road, Albany, North Shore NZ 0632
Phone: 0800 449 725

For learning solutions, visit **cengage.com.au**

Printed in Australia by Ligare Pty Ltd
6 7 8 9 10 11 12 20 19 18 17 16

Evaluated in independent research by staff from the Department of Language, Literacy and Arts Education at the University of Melbourne.

The Coat

Sharon Holt
Connah Brecon

Contents

Chapter 1

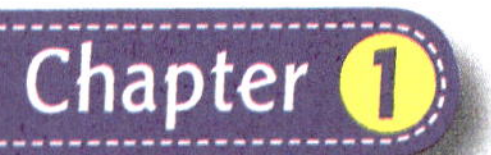

A Conversation

Mark knew he shouldn't be listening
under the window
at old Mr Crowe's house.
But he couldn't help it –
the voices were so loud.
Anyway, if he moved away now
he might be seen.

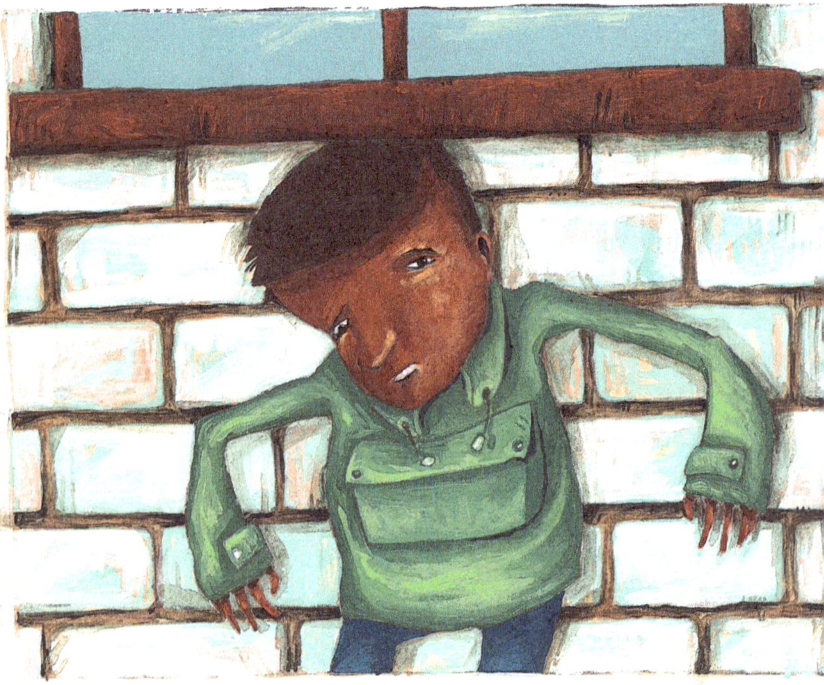

“What old coat?” asked a woman.

“The grey one, with all the pockets,” said a man, angrily.

That was Mr Crowe.

Then Mark heard the woman speak again.

"That old thing!" she laughed. "I put it out for the garbage truck this morning. It should have been thrown away years ago."

That must be Mr Crowe's daughter,
thought Mark.
She's the only one
who ever visits him.
As he thought about his neighbour,
Mark realised there was
a different noise
coming from the house.
The old man was sobbing.

"Why are you so upset?"
asked the woman.
"It was just an old coat."

The sobbing grew louder.
Mark couldn't move.
Then he heard the old man
speak again.

Running Words 154

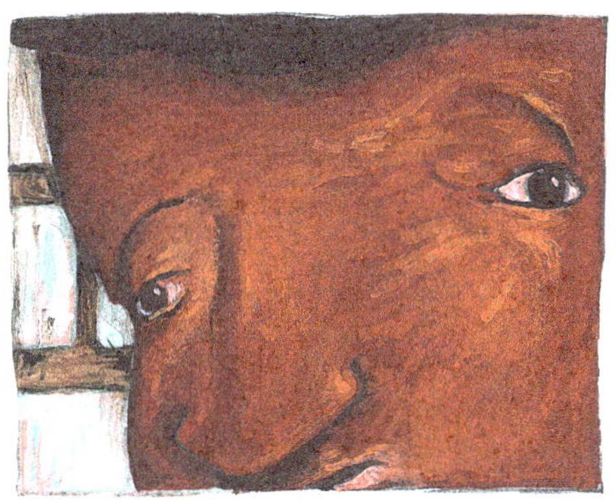

"It wasn't just an old coat,"
he shouted.
"The pockets were full of treasure!"

Mark's stomach lurched as he took in
what Mr Crowe had said.
He had to find the coat – fast.

The Garbage Truck

Mark had followed
the garbage truck before.
He looked at his watch.
By now, it would be going up
Hill Street.
There was still time to catch it
before it reached the dump.
He ran behind the shed
to get his bike.

"Where are you going?"
called his mother,
as he cycled past the kitchen window.

"Not far," shouted Mark.

Mark could feel the sweat
running down his back
as he cycled up Hill Road.
Each push of the pedal
seemed to repeat Mr Crowe's words.
"The pockets ... full of treasure.
The pockets ... full of treasure."

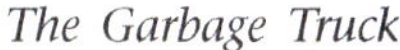

Mark wondered what could be
in the pockets.
Hundreds of dollars at least.
Maybe even thousands.
Or diamonds, emeralds and rubies.
The thought of it kept him going.

At last Mark reached the top
of the hill.
He could see the garbage truck,
not far from the dump.
He didn't think it would be hard
to spot Mr Crowe's trash bag.
Everyone else in the street used
plastic ties,
but Mr Crowe's bag was always
tied up with string –
just like the string the old man used
to hold up his trousers.

Mark started pedalling again.
He was going down the hill this time,
with his face into the wind.

Mark stopped behind the truck
as it turned off the road
and into the dump.

The driver unloaded the garbage
and drove away.

Mark cycled over to the pile of trash.
Where was the bag tied with string?
He couldn't see it anywhere.

Yuck.
He felt something ooze
under his shoe,
but he kept going.
Where was that bag?

Chapter 3

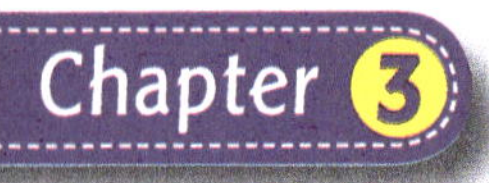

A Decision

Suddenly, Mark saw a piece of string. That must be it, he thought.

But how was he going to reach it through all the rubbish?

The smell was starting to make him feel sick.

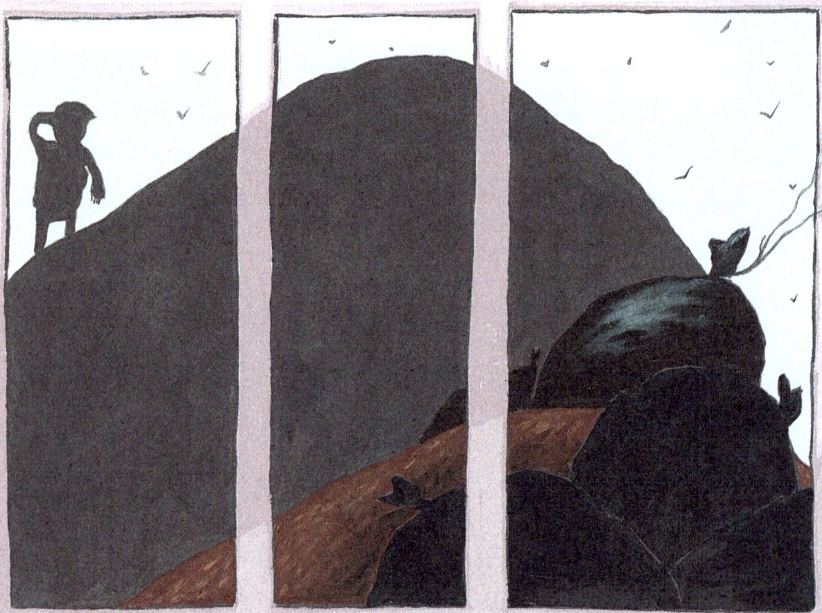

Finally, he reached it.
He untied the string,
and there was the coat,
at the top of the bag.
Mark pulled it out,
put it under his arm,
and picked up his bike.

At home, Mark's mother
was working on the computer.
"Hello," she called,
without looking up from her work.
"Everything all right?"

"Yes," said Mark. "Fine."
He went to his bedroom
and shut the door.

Mark spread out the coat
and emptied the pockets.
There was an old fob watch,
a faded photo of a young woman,
a locket, bottle tops
and a shark's tooth.
Mark checked through
the pockets again.
Where was the treasure?

Mark looked up when his mother came into the room.

“What’s all this?” she asked.

Mark looked away.
“Just some old stuff I found at the dump.”

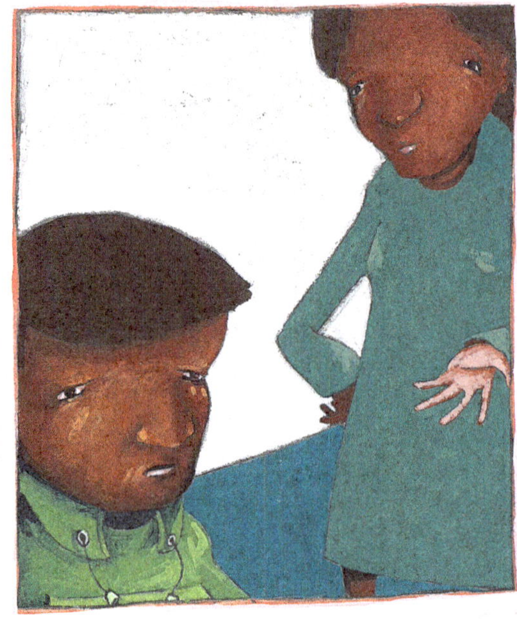

"It looks like someone's treasure," said his mother.
"Maybe they threw it away by mistake."

"Maybe," said Mark.

"Anyway," Mum said, "time for lunch."

Mark thought about Mr Crowe's treasure all afternoon.
He wasn't sure what to do with it.
Maybe he should take it back to the dump.

The next morning, Mark found Mr Crowe in his garden. Suddenly, Mark knew what to do.

"Hello," said Mark. "I found your coat."

The old man looked surprised as he took his coat from Mark. "How? Where?" he asked. Then, he looked at the faded photo. "You've made an old man very happy," he said.

"Good," smiled Mark.